FARCICALS

Two Short Farces

by Alan Ayckbourn

SAMUEL FRENCH

samuelfrench.co.uk

FOR AMATEUR PRODUCTION ENQUIRIES

UNITED KINGDOM AND WORLD
EXCLUDING NORTH AMERICA
plays@samuelfrench.co.uk
020 7255 4302/01

Each title is subject to availability from Samuel French, depending upon country of performance.

THINKING ABOUT PERFORMING A SHOW?

There are thousands of plays and musicals available to perform from Samuel French right now, and applying for a licence is easier and more affordable than you might think

---

From classic plays to brand new musicals, from monologues to epic dramas, there are shows for everyone.

Plays and musicals are protected by copyright law, so if you want to perform them, the first thing you'll need is a licence. This simple process helps support the playwright by ensuring they get paid for their work and means that you'll have the documents you need to stage the show in public.

Not all our shows are available to perform all the time, so it's important to check and apply for a licence before you start rehearsals or commit to doing the show.

LEARN MORE & FIND THOUSANDS OF SHOWS

Browse our full range of plays and musicals, and find out more about how to license a show
www.samuelfrench.co.uk/perform

Talk to the friendly experts in our Licensing team for advice on choosing a show and help with licensing
plays@samuelfrench.co.uk   020 7387 9373

Acting Editions

BORN TO PERFORM

Playscripts designed from the ground up to work the way you do in rehearsal, performance and study

---

Larger, clearer text for easier reading

Wider margins for notes

Performance features such as character and props lists, sound and lighting cues, and more

---

+ CHOOSE A SIZE AND STYLE TO SUIT YOU

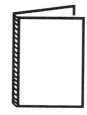

STANDARD EDITION

Our regular paperback book at our regular size

SPIRAL-BOUND EDITION

The same size as the Standard Edition, but with a sturdy, easy-to-fold, easy-to-hold spiral-bound spine

LARGE EDITION

A4 size and spiral bound, with larger text and a blank page for notes opposite every page of text – perfect for technical and directing use

---

LEARN MORE | samuelfrench.co.uk/actingeditions

Absent Friends

Arrivals and Departures

A Small Family Business

Awaking Beauty

Bedroom Farce

Body Language

Callisto 5

The Champion of Paribanou

A Chorus of Disapproval

Comic Potential

Communicating Doors

Confusions

A Cut in the Rates

Dreams from a Summer House

Drowning on Dry Land

Ernie's Incredible Illucinations

Mixed Doubles

Mr. A's Amazing Maze Plays

Mr Whatnot

My Very Own Story

My Wonderful Day

Neighbourhood Watch

The Norman Conquests: Table Manners; Living Together;
Round and Round the Garden

Private Fears in Public Places

Relatively Speaking

The Revengers' Comedies

RolePlay

Roundelay

Season's Greetings

Sisterly Feelings

Snake in the Grass

Suburban Strains

Sugar Daddies

Taking Steps

Ten Times Table

Things We Do for Love

This Is Where We Came In

Time and Time Again

Time of My Life

Tons of Money (revised)

Way Upstream

Wildest Dreams

Wolf at the Door

Woman in Mind

A Word from Our Sponsor

**Other plays by ALAN AYCKBOURN
licensed by Samuel French**

The Boy Who Fell Into a Book

Invisible Friends

The Jollies

Orvin – Champion of Champions

Surprises

Whenever

**FIND PERFECT PLAYS TO PERFORM AT
www.samuelfrench.co.uk/perform**

ABOUT THE AUTHOR

Alan Ayckbourn has worked in theatre as a playwright and director for over fifty years, rarely if ever tempted by television or film, which perhaps explains why he continues to be so prolific. To date he has written more than eighty plays, many one act plays and a large amount of work for the younger audience. His work has been translated into over thirty-five languages, is performed on stage and television throughout the world and has won countless awards.

Major successes include: *Relatively Speaking, How the Other Half Loves, Absurd Person Singular, Bedroom Farce, A Chorus of Disapproval,* and *The Norman Conquests.* In recent years, there have been revivals of *Season's Greetings* and *A Small Family Business* at the National Theatre; in the West End *Absent Friends, A Chorus of Disapproval, Relatively Speaking* and *How the Other Half Loves*; and at Chichester Festival Theatre, major revivals of *Way Upstream* in 2015, and *The Norman Conquests* in 2017.

Artistic Director of the Stephen Joseph theatre from 1972–2009, where almost all his plays have been first staged, he continues to direct his latest new work there. He has been inducted into American Theater's Hall of Fame, received the 2010 Critics' Circle Award for Services to the Arts and became the first British playwright to receive both Olivier and Tony Special Lifetime Achievement Awards. He was knighted in 1997 for services to the theatre.

Image credit: Andrew Higgins.

MUSIC USE NOTE

IMPORTANT BILLING AND CREDIT REQUIREMENTS

FARCICALS

Farcicals consists of two one-act plays, which ran individually and as a double bill during the premiere season and tour.

Farcicals World premiere (as double bill): 4 September 2013 at The McCarthy auditorium, Stephen Joseph Theatre, Scarborough

With the following cast:
Penny Bottlecamp ELIZABETH BOAG
Lottie Bulbin SARAH STANLEY
Teddy Bulbin, Lottie's husband TERENCE BOOTH*
Reggie Bottlecamp, Penny's husband KIM WALL

Director: ALAN AYCKBOURN
Design: JAN BEE BROWN
Costumes: JULIA PERRY-MOOK

---

* * Bill Champion took over the role of Teddy during the 2014 UK tour which premiered at the Yvonne Arnaud Theatre, Guildford on 24 January 2014, before being presented at the Brits Off Broadway festival, 59E59 theatres, New York, opening on 7th June, 2014.

CHARACTERS

PENNY BOTTLECAMP
LOTTIE BULBIN
TEDDY BULBIN – Lottie's husband
REGGIE BOTTLECAMP – Penny's husband

SETTING

An area of the Bulbin's country garden, during a summer evening.

THE
KIDDERMINSTER
AFFAIR

The **BULBIN**'s *garden in summer on a warm evening.*

An unlit barbecue is set up ready, together with garden seating and a table or two. **LOTTIE**, *small and anxious, enters with* **PENNY**, *tall and assured.*

PENNY *(as they enter)* ...I don't believe it. Lottie, are you sure? Are you certain you've got this right?

LOTTIE *(distraught)* Penny. I'm almost positive. I didn't want to believe it at first, but...

PENNY A love affair?

LOTTIE Yes.

PENNY What, <u>Teddy</u>?

LOTTIE I'm almost certain he's having one.

PENNY Well I'm – I'm knocked sideways. Lottie, this has absolutely hooked me for six... It's unbelievable!

LOTTIE *(miserably)* I just don't know what to do, Penny, I really don't. I'm sorry, I'm in a bit of a state. I've already had a drink or two to steady my nerves...

PENNY Yes, well do go easy, darling. You know what you're like after a drink or two. Listen, Lottie, have you told anyone else about this?

LOTTIE No. Only you. You're the first person I ran to. Instinctively. You're my one and only best friend and you have been ever since schooldays, haven't you? Ever since I was thirteen, I've turned to you in times of need. You've always been a pillar of strength for me, Penny, you know.

PENNY Yes, darling, and I'm still here for you.

LOTTIE Remember how you used to stand up for me at St Olaf's when I was being bullied...?

PENNY Now, that's all in the past now, Lottie, you have to forget that. Put it behind you, darling –

LOTTIE I never will, Penny. I'll never forget you standing up for me. You remember that time when they all started calling me Porky-pudge? The whole school. Do you remember that? Porky-pudge!

PENNY Children can be so cruel... Especially growing girls.

LOTTIE Porky-pudge. You know, I still wake up in the night sometimes to hear someone shouting in my ear... Porky-pudge! Porky-pudge!

PENNY Who on earth's shouting that, Teddy?

LOTTIE Teddy? Heavens, no! No, it's a voice in my dreams... Teddy does shout out in the night sometimes but nothing like that.

PENNY What does he shout? What sort of things?

LOTTIE Oh, he has these recurring horse riding dreams, apparently. He yells out, giddy up, old girl! And whooaa! Whoaa! Easy, now, easy!

PENNY Yes, that could get irritating after a time, I would imagine. Now getting back to this business of Teddy... How can you be so sure that he's having an affair, Lottie? How can you know for certain?

LOTTIE Well, he's frequently away for the occasional night and sometimes whole weekends, but then he's always done that. Ever since he diversified and went into lawn mowers. I mean, when he was just in tractors it wasn't quite so bad, but lawn mowers take him up and down the country continuously. Up and down, up and down, nearly every week.

PENNY And how do you know? About the affair?

LOTTIE You see, these trips have just got more and more frequent of late and he's away overnight far more than he used to be. And then the other night... I found...

PENNY You found what?

LOTTIE He...he gave me his suit...the pinstripe that he likes to wear when he's at mowing conventions and so on...he gave it to me to be cleaned...while he was away...and I was checking the pockets just to make sure, he hadn't left any... loose change...business cards...mobile phones and so on...

PENNY Yes, Lottie dear, what did you find?

LOTTIE I found... I found a bill.

PENNY A bill?

LOTTIE A hotel bill. From a Travelodge.

PENNY Go on.

LOTTIE In Kidderminster. Made out for Mr and Mrs Bulbin... One night with full English times two. He'd even used our married name, Penny...

PENNY *(involuntarily)* Oh the bloody idiot!

LOTTIE What?

PENNY *(angrily)* How can men be quite so idiotic? They're utterly thoughtless, aren't they? And I don't mean by thoughtless that they're inconsiderate, though they're that as well. I mean that they don't have a single thought in their stupid heads, do they? They just don't think at all! Use their tiny brains! They don't have a speck of intelligence, nothing! They never think of anyone but themselves!

She pauses, breathing deeply. Her burst of anger spent.
LOTTIE *is a little startled by her friend's vehemence.*

I'm sorry, Lottie, forgive me. That sort of behaviour gets me riled.

LOTTIE Obviously.

PENNY *(irritably)* Where are they, our two, anyway? What are they both doing?

LOTTIE They're in Teddy's study. Watching the cricket highlights.

PENNY Well, they should be out here. Getting this wretched barbecue ready. I suppose they're going to leave it all to us to do?

LOTTIE Oh, no. Not the barbecue. That's strictly Teddy's department. I couldn't possibly interfere, not with his barbecue...

PENNY No, it's an extraordinary thing about men, isn't it? Especially those that refuse point blank ever to set foot in a kitchen, men who would never dream of venturing within two feet of a stove and as for the sink – they simply run a mile. But as soon as a barbecue's mentioned, "No, no, better leave this to me, old girl. Men's work, don't you know? Tricky thing, grilling chunks of chicken, or charring a perfectly good steak beyond all recognition. Besides, it gets a teensy bit hot for your dainty little hands, dearest..." I mean it's still perfectly OK for us women to do all the hard work. Preparing and marinating, spending hours on end chopping up the wretched salads that none of the men bother to eat. And that we women are then left finishing up for weeks afterwards for breakfast. Perfectly acceptable for us to clear up the unholy mess they've left behind them afterwards... And then at the end of it, they expect us to stand here and bloody well applaud, "Jolly well done, darling, bravo, delicious!" Well sod them, that's what I say, sod the lot of them!

LOTTIE *(nervously)* Gracious! You are in a mood today, Penny. What on earth's wrong? Is there something wrong?

PENNY I'm angry for you, darling. For you.

LOTTIE I can't bear the thought of that happening in some Travelodge. I know, I tell myself sometimes that I'm terribly lucky to have him in the first place. God knows why he chose me out of all the... He could have had the pick of us, couldn't he? ...All my friends were green with jealousy. "Why you, Lottie?" they kept saying. "What on earth made him choose you?" They were mystified. They were all in love with him, too, of course, every single one of them. Even you, Penny, I remember at one point.

PENNY Me? No, no, no. I never was. Me?

LOTTIE Oh, come now, Penny, I remember you giving him sheep's eyes...

PENNY He's not my type. Teddy's not my type. Not at all. Teddy? All that alpha male swagger. All that surface charm...tall, good looking, superficially sexually attractive men – they're ten a penny, aren't they? No, give me Reggie...any time. Reggie's much more – my type of man. No disrespect to Teddy, but with my men I like to look below the surface a bit – in the hope there's something there. With Reggie, if you dig deep enough, eventually you're sure to find something interesting. That's my hope, anyway.

LOTTIE Yes. I think Reggie's really sort of deep, isn't he? He always comes over as deep. A bit of a philosopher. He always gives you that intense, penetrating stare when you talk to him, doesn't he? As if he's analysing every word you're saying to him...

PENNY He's probably trying to work out what you're talking about. Listen, Lottie. If you want to keep that husband of yours, you're going to have to take positive action, dear.

LOTTIE Positive action? What sort of positive action?

PENNY Start up a love affair of your own, darling. Give him a taste of what it's like to be on the receiving end. They don't like that, they never do.

LOTTIE (*flustered*) Oh, no I couldn't...me? I could never...not in a Travelodge in Kidderminster. Can you see me...? With some...? No, I couldn't, Penny, I really couldn't.

PENNY You don't have to go the whole hog with him. You don't have to go all the way, do you...?

LOTTIE Not all the...? You mean, just sort of take my top off for him, that sort of thing –?

PENNY Maybe not even that. Flirt, darling, you remember how to flirt, don't you? Remember the old sheep's eyes, you used to give Teddy? Try them on another man. Start working the old magic again, Lottie.

LOTTIE Oh, I don't –

PENNY Come on, darling, you can do it! God! It worked well enough with Teddy, didn't it? Whatever you did to him, dear, you saw off the field, didn't you? You showed the rest of us a clean pair of heels?

LOTTIE *(laughing nervously)* I don't think I did anything with Teddy as far as I can remember. I just kept dropping things and falling over, mostly. I got so terribly nervous when I was with him, you see. Terrified. He was always picking things up for me. Helping me back on my feet, dusting me down, you know. He was very considerate, in those days. Now he just tends to sit there and shout "Whoops" or "Clumsy!".

PENNY If you want him back, darling, my advice is to give it a go. You know Lottie, I have to say, I'd hate to think that this woman – whoever she is – would endanger your marriage. That was never her intention. I presume. She probably just fancied a fling, that's all. A taste of – something she was unable to taste before.

LOTTIE A taste of Teddy?

PENNY If you like. But now she's tasted – that's – in all probability – satisfied her inner craving...so, as far as she's concerned, this woman, she's probably popped him safely back in the fridge, her pangs satisfied.

LOTTIE This all sounds very distasteful. I don't think I'd care to meet this woman. Her hands all over Teddy, treating him like some sort of midnight snack.

PENNY The point I'm making, if you don't want him roving elsewhere, is you need to win him back. Reclaim as your own. The next time you're out with him together somewhere in public, the first man who gives you a second glance, doesn't matter who he is, you give it a go, darling. Sheep's eyes, remember.

LOTTIE Well, I'll try. It's only, if it came to it, I'm not sure I could – I'm so rusty –

PENNY Ah! Here they are! At last. Not a word about any of this.

LOTTIE No. Any of what?

TEDDY *and* **REGGIE** *enter.*

TEDDY, *assured and confident.*

REGGIE, *his friend, slightly less so.*

They both carry drinks. **TEDDY** *also carries a half full red wine bottle.*

TEDDY *(as they enter)* Alright! Help is at hand! Here we are. Stand well back, girls! Barbecue is imminent! T minus ten and counting!

PENNY Thank God! About time!

TEDDY We'll take over from here, won't we Reggie?

REGGIE Oh, yes. Leave it all to us.

LOTTIE We'll bring things down, then. It's all ready.

TEDDY I'll get this thing fired up...

PENNY *(dryly)* Oh, dear! We girls had better keep well back, then!

REGGIE *(laughing)* Yes, you better had! You alright, darling?

PENNY Fine. It would have been especially nice though if you'd poured us both a drink, don't you think, darling?

REGGIE Oh, sorry. Never occurred to me...

TEDDY It's all there on the sitting room sideboard – help yourselves, girls! There's everything you could possibly want from Baileys to Babycham, eh? *(He laughs)*

REGGIE *laughs.*

PENNY *laughs mirthlessly.*

LOTTIE *(smiling awkwardly)* Yes, I'll fix us one, Penny.

PENNY I'll have a very large gin, thank you, Lottie. Do excuse us, boys, we're off to do the hard work now.

REGGIE Righty-ho!

LOTTIE Was the cricket good?

TEDDY		No. Bloody disaster. Total
	(Speaking together)	collapse.
REGGIE		Dreadful. Complete washout. Hopeless bunch.

LOTTIE Oh, dear. How disappointing. Maybe they need some new men?

PENNY Somebody does, certainly.

LOTTIE *(nervously)* Yes. Well come on, Penny. We'll leave them to it, shall we?

PENNY Lead on, darling.

The women move off. LOTTIE *trips and nearly falls.*

LOTTIE *(regaining her balance)* Oh!

TEDDY *(engaged with the barbecue)* Whoops!

REGGIE *(rushing to her)* You, alright, Lottie?

LOTTIE *(smiling at him)* Yes, I'm fine, thank you Reggie. It's just these stupid shoes, I don't know why I wore them, really...

PENNY *(as they leave)* They're rather sweet, I've been admiring them. Where on earth did you get them...?

LOTTIE *(as they leave)* Oh, there's quite a story behind these shoes...

Both women go off.

TEDDY Hark at that! Women and shoes! Fatal! I often say
to Lottie, thank God you don't have another pair of legs,
woman, or you'd completely bankrupt us!

They both laugh.

REGGIE Another pair of legs, that's very good...

TEDDY Thank God for a sense of humour, eh?

REGGIE British sense of humour. Nothing like it. Famous, isn't
it? You know I sometimes have nightmares where I dream
I'm foreign and then I wake up and I think, thank God!

TEDDY Foreign? What sort of foreign?

REGGIE I never know. It tends to vary. All I know is, I can't
speak very good English. People keep shouting at me.

TEDDY Very odd. Right, let's get underway. If you can hand
things to me, Reggie, if you don't mind?

REGGIE Yes, of course.

TEDDY Right, pass me a few of those briquettes, would you?
In the bag there?

REGGIE Briquettes, coming up. There you go. Sound rather
like an all girl dance troupe, don't they? The Briquettes?

TEDDY *(laughing)* Oh yes, rather square shaped girls.

REGGIE Square dancers, perhaps?

They both roar with laughter. REGGIE *passes* TEDDY *a
few briquettes from a sack.*

More?

TEDDY Yes. Keep 'em coming, Reggie.

REGGIE *passes* TEDDY *more.*

(as they do this) Oh, it's good to be with you, old boy. Have
a laugh with someone who's like minded. Another chap.

You can't really laugh with a woman, can you? Well, not in the same way.

REGGIE No, I don't think I laugh a lot with Penny.

TEDDY I don't imagine you would do, no.

REGGIE She tends to take most of my jokes rather seriously. Just stares at me, faintly incredulous.

TEDDY No, they don't share the same sense of humour as us, do they?

REGGIE No. Very rarely. And, then again – here's an interesting one – on the occasions when I'm being perfectly serious, when I'm not making jokes at all, I suddenly catch Penny roaring with laughter. Rolling on the floor.

TEDDY Mysterious lot. Now, look at this. This is your basic briquette pyramid, you see? And then into the middle of this, strategically positioned, I'm going to place equidistantly three of those firelighters over there...

REGGIE *(reaching for them)* Just three?

TEDDY Just three. Not two. Not four. But three. *(Accepting them)* Ta. *(Indicating)* Just like this, see? Equidistantly placed.

REGGIE Bit of a precise science this, isn't it?

TEDDY It is.

REGGIE I must say I just tend to throw everything in, light a match, slam the lid and hope for the best.

TEDDY My God! What on earth does it all taste like at the end of it?

REGGIE Absolutely foul. Penny refuses to eat it and we usually end up going out to dinner.

TEDDY Well, wait till you've tried this. I promise you the most delicious, succulent steak, cooked to within a microsecond of perfection.

REGGIE Can't wait for that.

TEDDY Right. Pass that lighter. Thank you. Now.

He lights each of the firelighters.

Light blue touch paper...there we go...

REGGIE *(watching, fascinated)* The big moment. Bravo.

TEDDY And hey presto. Ignition!

REGGIE That's done the trick.

TEDDY We're away.

> **TEDDY** *replaces the grill.*

Must remember to brush this with oil, too. Vegetable oil. Before we put the steaks on. Otherwise they stick.

REGGIE Oh yes, mine do that.

TEDDY Yours stick?

REGGIE Any steak I've cooked tends to arrive in shreds. House speciality. Shreddy a la Reggie.

> **TEDDY** *closes the lid. The faint sounds of crackling and spluttering as the briquttes heat up. Occasional wafts of smoke seep from the vents.*

TEDDY *(contentedly)* Leave that for a bit. Now, where's that drink?

REGGIE There.

TEDDY Oh yes. Top up?

REGGIE Oh yes, don't mind if I do. Jolly good wine this.

> **TEDDY** *tops up* **REGGIE***'s glass and then his own.*

TEDDY Think so? It should be. I know a chap who knows the chap who grows it. Or rather he knows the chap who knows the chap who grows it. Cheers, old boy.

REGGIE Cheers. Here's to the chap who grows it.

They sit.

So how are you both? You and Lottie? Doesn't feel like we've seen you for ages. Considering we live practically next door... So how are you both? OK?

TEDDY Ah, you know, rubbing along fairly happily. You know.

REGGIE I thought Lottie was looking a bit fraught just now.

TEDDY Was she? Maybe she'd had a couple. She tends to do that occasionally of late.

REGGIE Really? That's a bit worrying isn't it? Come to that, Penny was a bit het up, as well.

TEDDY Maybe she'd had a couple, too?

REGGIE No. I don't think so. Not Penny. Not a secret drinker. Not Penny. If she decides to get drunk, she does it extremely publicly.

TEDDY Yes, I can imagine.

They both laugh. A silence.

And how are you both? You and Penny?

REGGIE Oh, pretty good, you know.

TEDDY Good.

Pause.

REGGIE We had a moment – a while back. A brief moment. A bump in the road. When we...but it blew over, thank God.

TEDDY A moment? What sort of moment?

REGGIE Well, frankly there was a moment when I actually thought she might be having an affair.

TEDDY Oh, yes?

REGGIE But, as I say, it turned out to be nothing at all.

TEDDY Nothing at all?

REGGIE Oh no. Absolutely nothing at all.

TEDDY Thank God!

REGGIE Sorry?

TEDDY Thank God it wasn't true.

REGGIE Oh, rather. Thank God!

> **TEDDY** *gets up to check the barbecue. He lifts the lid. Some smoke.*

TEDDY Yes, that's heating up nicely.

REGGIE No, it all hinged around an incident in Kidderminster.

> **TEDDY** *drops the lid of the barbecue rather too vigorously. A lot of smoke. He chokes.*

TEDDY Kidderminster!

REGGIE *(rather startled)* Yes. Kidderminster. Anything wrong?

TEDDY *(coughing and eyes watering)* No, no. I thought – for a minute one of the briquettes had failed to catch but – carry on... Kidderminster, you say?

REGGIE Yes, she was apparently seen by Charlie Withers, a colleague of mine from the showroom, she was creeping into some hotel in Kidderminster. He was out test driving this Lamborghini with some client.

TEDDY A Lamborghini?

REGGIE Yes. Canary yellow. Lovely car.

TEDDY Test driving a Lamborghini? In the middle of Kidderminster?

REGGIE Yes. The customer was apparently interested in its town fuel consumption as compared to a Ford Fiesta.

TEDDY How did it compare?

REGGIE Not very favourably, I'm afraid. Those vehicles are never very happy going at less than seventy. Preferably on a disused air field. Anyway, as it happens, Charlie stalled it just outside this Travelodge and there was Penny apparently slinking in. To all intents as of a woman in pursuit of a secret assignation.

TEDDY Oh, my God. Did you ask her about it?

REGGIE To my shame, Teddy, I confess I did. What, I asked her in fairly stern tones – well, as stern as you can ever get with Penny – what were you doing creeping into a Travelodge in Kidderminster at six o'clock on a Saturday evening?

TEDDY What did she say to that?

REGGIE Well, she choked back a tear – you know Penny she never cries, she's not that sort of woman –

TEDDY No. Not often.

REGGIE – she choked back a tear and said, "Well, the secret's out. You've ruined everything now, you blithering idiot!" Her precise words.

TEDDY They were?

REGGIE She'd apparently had a secret assignation with the manager.

TEDDY With the manager as well? As well as this – other person.

REGGIE The manager of the Travelodge. Apparently she'd been arranging a birthday surprise for me in time for next November, which I'd now gone and completely wrecked. She had it all arranged, a romantic evening for two, candle lit dinner, bed and breakfast, complimentary tea, coffee, hot chocolate, biscuits, so on and so on... In one of their very best rooms. I tell you, Teddy, I felt a complete louse. How could I ever have thought it of her? I felt thoroughly ashamed. She had to cancel it straightaway, of course.

TEDDY She did?

REGGIE Well, what was the point? Where was the surprise? So we're staying put at home. She offered to set up something else but I said to her, no, why bother? I'll doubtless only go and spoil that as well. I'll probably end up taking her out to dinner just to make it up to her, poor darling. You know, Teddy, I don't think I truly appreciate what I've got in that woman. I wake up sometimes and there she is, in the bed beside me, most nights, anyway, curled up, making these funny little noises –

TEDDY What sort of noises?

REGGIE Well, they're sort of whinnying noises, really. A bit like a horse, you know. God knows what she's dreaming about, bless her. But I hope I feature in it somewhere.

TEDDY Very possibly. *(Proffering the bottle)* Want to help me out to finish this, do you?

REGGIE My pleasure.

TEDDY *replenishes both their glasses.*

Ah, now come on. You haven't been totally frank with me, have you, Teddy? I've let you into my guilty secrets. What about yours?

TEDDY How do you mean?

REGGIE When I first mentioned Kidderminster, you jumped like a scalded cat. Now, what was that all about? What's all this with you and Kidderminster?

TEDDY Well. It's a – it's a long and complicated story, Reggie. Old chap.

A silence. REGGIE *waits.* TEDDY *thinks and clears his throat.*

Extremely complicated.

REGGIE *waits.* TEDDY *clears his throat again.*

I'll just check on that barbecue.

TEDDY *checks the barbecue. More smoke. He recoils and chokes.*

Yes, that's fine. All's well.

REGGIE Good. And?

TEDDY And what?

REGGIE I'm still waiting to hear the end of this long and extremely complicated story of yours.

TEDDY Oh, God! Oh that! Slipped my mind, sorry. It's a perfectly simple story really. Not at all complicated. Perfectly straightforward. It's something that happened to Lottie and me. When we were still newly-weds we had an incident in Kidderminster – which we rather want to put behind us regarding a – it's funny that your incident involved cars. So did ours.

REGGIE Yours involved a car, as well?

TEDDY Coincidence.

REGGIE You and Lottie?

TEDDY Yes, we had a very unpleasant occurrence involving a slow puncture which left us both rather traumatised, I'm afraid. And it's something we both prefer not to talk about, if you don't mind. In fact, Lottie particularly gets very, very upset at the mention of the word.

REGGIE Slow puncture?

TEDDY Kidderminster.

REGGIE Oh, Kidderminster? *(Thoughtfully)* I see. Kidderminster.

TEDDY *(wincing)* Ah! Yes, you can see I'm not completely over it either. So please don't mention it, Reggie, if you don't mind. We're both still having a hard time coming to terms with it – Lottie frequently goes completely to pieces at the very mention of the word.

REGGIE Kidderminster.

TEDDY *(wincing)* Ah!

REGGIE Sorry, old boy. I do beg your pardon. I won't bring it up again. Must have been one hell of a slow puncture.

TEDDY Yes, it was.

REGGIE Well, take my tip. This is the professional car salesman in me talking now, you understand, you really ought to ensure you carry a spare.

TEDDY *(returning to check the barbecue)* Yes, I do. These days I always make sure I've got a spare.

REGGIE Ah, here they come, bless them. Goddesses bearing goodies.

> **PENNY**, *slightly drunk, enters with a laden tray of prepared but as yet uncooked food including marinated steaks. As she enters, there is the sound of a crash from behind her, off, as* **LOTTIE** *drops her own tray.*

LOTTIE *(offstage)* Oh, damn, damn, damn! Bugger! Bugger! Bugger!

TEDDY *(still at the barbecue)* Whoops! Clumsy!

REGGIE *(alarmed)* Are you OK, Lottie?

LOTTIE *(offstage)* No!

PENNY I knew that would happen, the minute she picked it up, I could see it coming.

REGGIE *(hurrying offstage)* Just a tick, Lottie! Help is at hand!

> **REGGIE** *goes offstage.*

> **PENNY** *puts her own tray on the table and starts to unload it.*

TEDDY What has she dropped now, for God's sake?

PENNY The other half of the meal.

TEDDY Please, God. Not the steaks, I hope. Cost a fortune.

PENNY No, they're with me. She had the trifle.

TEDDY How many's she had?

PENNY I lost count after the seventh glass. She's in a bit of a state, actually, Teddy. I really think you ought to do something.

TEDDY State? What sort of state?

A bellow of laughter from off from **LOTTIE** *and* **REGGIE**.

PENNY *gives a swift look in their directions and then continues at the table.*

PENNY *(cryptically)* I think she's a little upset about the cricket.

TEDDY *(disbelievingly)* The cricket? Lottie?

PENNY Yes, you see she's just discovered that her captain apparently has been moonlighting with another team.

TEDDY I don't – oh! Oh, yes. Has he? Has she? Has she any idea which other team?

PENNY No, not yet. But if you have anything to do with it, Teddy, it'll only be a matter of time before she does. I think we're going to have to cancel all future away fixtures, aren't we?

TEDDY Yes, quite. Quite. That's a shame.

More laughter from offstage.

What happens now, then?

PENNY Well, to continue in cricketing parlance, we're simply going to have to bite the bullet and reorganise our respective batting line ups, aren't we?

TEDDY I see.

PENNY If you take my advice, as far as you're concerned, Teddy, you'd better start by reinstating your original opening pair.

REGGIE *enters with the second tray, obviously much denuded.*

TEDDY *starts to put on his chef's apron.*

REGGIE Here we are, the best of what's left of it.

PENNY Just been saying to Teddy how disappointing it was about the cricket.

REGGIE Really? I didn't know you were that interested.

PENNY I enjoy the occasional game, that's all. Where's Lottie?

REGGIE She's coming. She's just scraping trifle off the carpet in there. What shall I do with this?

PENNY *(indicating the other table)* Oh, just put it down there for now. Is any of it still edible?

REGGIE *(putting down his tray)* Not much. Unless you fancy picking your way through carpet fluff. She seems – Lottie seems quite – heightened this evening. If you know what I mean. Bit on the over-friendly side. I don't think I've ever seen that aspect of her before. Keeps giving me these strange looks – bit like a stricken lamb...

PENNY Oh, my God! Now what have I started?

> **LOTTIE** *enters, rather flushed and red-faced and rather drunk.*

LOTTIE Thank you so much. You're a dear man, Reggie. You really are a gentleman, you know, helping me like that.

> **LOTTIE** *favours him with a rather fixed smile and wide-eyed facial expression which is her own version of sheep's eyes.*

REGGIE *(retreating slightly)* That's quite alright, Lottie. My pleasure.

PENNY Lottie, dear, do sit down. Before you fall down again, darling.

LOTTIE No, Penny, I want to talk to Reggie. Because Reggie's a gentleman. Don't you agree, Penny?

PENNY *(as she goes offstage)* Yes, he can be. Occasionally.

LOTTIE I prefer talking to gentlemen. Rather than other persons present. People who, when a lady drops something just shout "whoops clumsy!" They aren't gentlemen. I don't mind saying, I find gentlemen very attractive. Very, very attractive indeed.

She favours **REGGIE** *with another of her looks. He laughs nervously.*

REGGIE *(nervously)* Oh, lord! Sorry about this, Teddy.

TEDDY For god's sake, Lottie, simmer down, woman!

LOTTIE Don't you talk to me like that, you – beastly barbecuing Bulbin!

TEDDY Right, I think you've had more than enough to drink, darling! As soon as I've put these steaks on, I'm putting you to bed, Lottie.

LOTTIE Bed? I'm not going to bed with you, Teddy! I know who I'm going to bed with and it certainly won't be you, Mr Bossyboots! Reggie!

She favours **REGGIE** *with another of her looks.* **TEDDY** *starts hastily oiling the grill, using a brush which he dips in a small bowl of vegetable oil.* **REGGIE** *retreats in order to escape* **LOTTIE**'s *wide-eyed assault.*

REGGIE Oh, good grief! *(Moving to a table to examine the food)* Aha! Now, what goodies have we here, then?

LOTTIE *follows* **REGGIE**.

LOTTIE *(sweetly)* I'm sure there's something here you'd fancy, Reggie? Everything's home made, you know...

REGGIE Oh, splendid...

LOTTIE *(moving increasingly closer to him, seductively)* There's all sorts of salads. Lemony potato salad, tomato, cucumber and coriander salad, baked goat's cheese with tomato vinaigrette salad, fennel and pepper salad... Do any of those attract you at all, Reggie?

PENNY *re-enters.*

REGGIE *(retreating nervously)* Goodness, what a choice! Salad heaven!

PENNY Lottie, now stop that! Teddy, do hurry up with those steaks...

LOTTIE Avocado and citrus salad – yum-yum – parsnip, carrot and ginger salad – oooh! – and Grandma Wiseman's English pea salad – *(She smacks her lips)* – Elizabethan herb and flower salad with honey dressing...

REGGIE *(nervously)* Yes, I daresay I could tackle the odd lottice leaf, Lettie. I mean lattice loaf, Lotsie... *(He laughs)*

LOTTIE *(with a peal of laughter)* Oh, Reggie, you're so silly!

> **LOTTIE** *picks out a long lettuce leaf from a salad.*

(holding out the leaf) Would you like me to feed you, Reggie? Like a rabbit? Would you like me to feed you, Reggie rabbit?

REGGIE *(nervously humouring her)* Yes, yes...that'd be lovely. Thank you. *(To the others)* I may need a spot of help here, you two.

LOTTIE *(poking the leaf at him)* Here! Here! Reggie Rabbit! Come and have a nibble! Come and have a nibble, then...

REGGIE *(to the others)* Any time now, please...

PENNY Teddy!

TEDDY Coming, just coming...

> *He has placed the steaks on the grill and now closes the lid.* **LOTTIE** *meanwhile has started to suck the lettuce leaf.*

LOTTIE Yum – yum...it's really lovely lettuce, delicious, finger-licking lettuce, yum-yum –

REGGIE Yes, it looks lovely... Where did you buy such lovely lettuce?

LOTTIE Oh, I got it from that little lettuce shop –

REGGIE Oh, which little lettuce shop was that?

LOTTIE Tesco's. The one in Kidderminster... *(She bursts into tears)* Oh, God! I can't do this any more! Penny! I can't do this, I'm so sorry, Reggie! I'm sorry, everybody!

LOTTIE buries her head in REGGIE's chest and clings to him. The others rise and move as if to prise LOTTIE away from REGGIE.

REGGIE *(with sudden realisation)* Oh, my God! I see! Of course!

TEDDY Darling, come on now...

PENNY Lottie, dear, that's enough...

REGGIE *(holding up a hand to stop them)* It's alright! It's alright! Leave this to me.

TEDDY I'll take her indoors. Put her to bed. Come on, darling, I'll put you to bed.

LOTTIE *(wailing)* I'm sorry.

PENNY Lottie!

PENNY and TEDDY move in together in an attempt to grab LOTTIE and prise her away from REGGIE.

Lottie, dear, come along now...

TEDDY Lottie, come on, old girl, upstairs...

REGGIE draws LOTTIE to him protectively and fends off the others in a burst of sudden uncharacteristic, protective authority.

REGGIE *(authoritatively)* No, no, leave her to me, please! Stand back! Now, stand well clear, both of you!

PENNY and TEDDY step back, startled.

I think I know what's happening here, Teddy. This is a lot more serious than you led me to believe.

TEDDY Is it?

REGGIE She said that word and it set her off, immediately.

PENNY What word? You mean, Tesco's?

REGGIE No, not that word. The other word.

PENNY Sainsbury's?

REGGIE No, come on, darling, this is no joking matter. A woman's health is at stake, here. Now, Lottie, you sit down! *(He sits her in a chair)* There! Everyone else stand back and sit down! Give her air. We're all going to talk this thing through now, face it together...

PENNY Talk what through? What's he talking about?

REGGIE Penny, do sit down, please.

TEDDY No idea. I've completely lost the thread.

REGGIE Everyone, sit down please! I absolutely insist!

TEDDY Lottie ought to be lying down.

PENNY *(sitting)* Oh, Teddy, just sit and do as he says. It's useless arguing with Reggie when he gets like this...

TEDDY *sits reluctantly-near to the barbecue.*

REGGIE *draws up a chair and sits close to* LOTTIE. *Slight pause.*

REGGIE Thank you. Now. Lottie has a problem and we're here to help her overcome it.

PENNY *(suspiciously)* What problem?

TEDDY Haven't the faintest idea.

REGGIE Now, now! I think you do, Teddy. As you said earlier, it's partly your problem too, isn't it, old boy? Be honest, now.

PENNY What's going on? *(Sharply to* TEDDY*)* What have you been telling him?

TEDDY I haven't told him anything.

REGGIE He's told me enough. About his – unfortunate incident at – *(With a glance at* **LOTTIE***)* Uh-huh-huh-huh…early on in their marriage…

PENNY Uh-huh-huh-huh? What on earth's Uh-huh-huh-huh?

REGGIE I'm afraid I'm unable to say the actual word because of… *(Indicating* **LOTTIE***)* …Nnn – nnn – but suffice it to say, it's to do with a slow – Sssssss! – which was apparently extremely traumatic for them both…and the whole thing happened at… Uh-huh-huh-huh.

TEDDY *(realising where this is leading)* Oh, God!

LOTTIE *(suddenly perking up and taking interest)* What's he talking about? Sssssss? Uh-huh-huh-huh? What's Uh-huh-huh-huh?

PENNY I do apologise, my husband's gone completely potty, Lottie.

TEDDY I think I know now what he's talking about.

PENNY You do?

TEDDY And I don't think, Reggie, it's a good idea to carry on with the topic of – Sssss, old boy. The slow Sssss in Uh-huh-huh-huh. Not in front of – *(Indicating* **LOTTIE***)* Nnn – nnn. *(Opening the barbecue lid)* Oh, yes these are coming on a treat… Soon be there.

LOTTIE No, no! I want to hear more about this. What all this about this slow Sssssss in Uh-huh-huh-huh?

REGGIE It's better if you're not reminded of it, Lottie.

TEDDY How does everyone like theirs cooked?

LOTTIE What are you talking about? Reminded of what?

TEDDY Rare? Medium rare?

REGGIE This is all very tricky and I'm going to do my very best not to hurt anyone's feelings, especially *(Indicating* **LOTTIE***)* Nnn-nn's…

TEDDY Well done?

REGGIE Thanks very much. Now, Nnn-nn – Sorry, I mean now, Lottie. *(Slowly to her as if to a child)* This concerns an incident, a motoring incident, which happened to you and Teddy early on in your marriage. Do you recall it?

LOTTIE I haven't the faintest idea what you're talking about. What's he talking about, Teddy?

PENNY I'll have mine rare please, Teddy, the rarer the better.

REGGIE Now, Lottie, I'm going to say two words to you now. Two words.

TEDDY Right, that's one rare. Any more takers?

REGGIE And I want you to take a deep breath before I say them to you. Will you do that? Deep breath, now.

LOTTIE *takes a deep breath.*

That's it. Well done. *(Carefully)* Now listen to the words, Lottie, here they come. Slow puncture.

LOTTIE *(mystified)* Slow puncture?

REGGIE Is that at all significant to you, Lottie?

TEDDY Reggie, I beg you not to pursue this any further, old chap –

REGGIE Just a minute, Teddy. I'm talking to *(indicating* **LOTTIE***)* Nnn-nn. I promise not to mention Uh-huh-huh-huh – Now, Lottie, does slow puncture not bring back memories at all?

LOTTIE No.

REGGIE No? She's obviously blocked it out, Teddy. Amazing thing the mind, isn't it? When you think of it. If something becomes too much for it. It just shuts it off. Miraculous.

PENNY I wish to God there was a way to shut yours off.

REGGIE No, no, it's really remarkable. *(He laughs)* Well, that's a relief if – *(Indicating* **LOTTIE***)* – Nn-nn's over the slow

Sssss, anyway. That's progress. Now it can be told. This whole thing stemmed originally, Penny, from something I was telling Teddy about us two. You know about your surprise...

PENNY Surprise? What surprise?

REGGIE The surprise you arranged for me in – Uh-huh-huh-huh.

TEDDY Look, I really wouldn't carry on with this, Reggie...

REGGIE With the Lamborghini. Remember? Canary yellow? In Uh-huh-huh-huh?

PENNY *(cottoning on)* Uh-huh-huh-huh? *(With a nervous glance at* **LOTTIE***)* Oh my god, you don't mean, Uh-huh-huh-huh?

REGGIE Yes, Uh-huh-huh-huh. The day Charlie saw Penny going into the –

PENNY *(cutting in swiftly)* Oh yes of course. When I was going into the Ah-ah-hah.

REGGIE The Ah-ah-hah?

PENNY Yes, darling, the Ah-ah-hah.

REGGIE I'm getting a bit lost here. Why on earth are we calling it that? The Ah-ah-hah? Why can't we just call it the –?

PENNY *(with an anxious look at* **LOTTIE***)* Darling, it's our secret. We don't want everyone to know about it, surely?

REGGIE Why not? Practically everyone knows, anyway. I mean you and I know and Teddy knows, the manager of the Ah-ah-hah knows and Charlie Withers certainly knows. I just don't see why we're calling it the Ah-ah-hah, all of a sudden.

LOTTIE What is going on here? Why are you all talking in code?

REGGIE Now don't panic, Lottie, there's no need to start panicking!

LOTTIE First there's Uh-huh-huh-huh and Sssss! and Nn-nn, now there's this Ah-ah-hah. I want to know what this Ah-ah-hah is. I demand to know!

REGGIE Oh no, damn it. I don't care. There's no harm in Nn-nn knowing about the Ah-ah-hah. I mean, I know she may still have a problem with Uh-huh-huh-huh but she's over the Sssss! And as far as we know she certainly doesn't have a problem with the Ah-ah-hah.

TEDDY *(swiftly)* Yes, she does!

PENNY *(simultaneously)* She certainly does!

REGGIE Oh dear heaven. She doesn't have a problem with the Ah-ah-hah, as well, does she? What on earth can have happened to her there? It can't have been the scene of the Sssss!, can it?

LOTTIE Happened to me where? <u>Where</u>?

REGGIE At the Travelodge – Oh, God, sorry – I've blown it – Sorry!

LOTTIE *(blankly)* Travelodge? The Travelodge?

REGGIE Oh, Lord, you were right. Nn-nn's obviously had a bad experience there, too.

PENNY How are those steaks doing?

TEDDY *(opening the barbecue briefly)* Oh, yes, coming on a treat!

LOTTIE Charlie saw Penny going into the Travelodge?

REGGIE That's right. Well done. She's getting there.

TEDDY What about another drink, everyone?

PENNY Super.

LOTTIE Penny going into a Travelodge in Uh-huh-huh-huh?

REGGIE Nearly there. She's piecing it together.

LOTTIE Uh-huh-huh-huh? Let me guess. Littlehampton?

REGGIE Close.

LOTTIE Uh-huh-huh-huh? Bishop's Stortford? Cirencester? Uh-huh-huh-huh? Oh, yes! Kidderminster!

REGGIE Well done! Clever girl! She's said the word! I think your problems are over, Teddy, old boy!

LOTTIE *casts her eyes round from* **REGGIE** *to* **TEDDY** *and finally to* **PENNY**, *as the whole thing falls into place.*

LOTTIE *(as she does this)* Kidderminster... Travelodge... Kidderminster... *(A slow mirthless laugh)* Ho-ho-ho-ho-ho...

REGGIE *(sotto)* Sorry, I'm afraid I haven't a clue what that stands for.

She rises and picks up the bowl of mayonnaise. She approaches **PENNY** *who is still seated. They all watch* **LOTTIE** *transfixed.*

LOTTIE *(slowly)* Ha-ha-ha-ha-ha... Kidderminster... *(Quietly to* **PENNY**) He-he-he-he! You treacherous, calculating, deceitful hussy!

She empties the bowl into **PENNY**'s *lap.*

PENNY *sits there motionless, barely reacting.*

TEDDY *(nervously)* Whoops! Clumsy!

REGGIE Oh, gosh!

PENNY *(quietly)* Alright, dear, you've made your point. You've got your own back. You've totally ruined a perfectly good dress of which I was extremely fond and I hope you're satisfied, Lottie.

LOTTIE *returns the empty bowl to the table. She picks up the bowl of salsa and weighs it in her hand.*

LOTTIE *(softly)* No, I'm not satisfied. I'm not at all satisfied.

TEDDY *(sensing big trouble)* Steady on, Lottie! Easy girl. Whooaa there!

LOTTIE *moves back and confronts* **PENNY**.

PENNY I warn you, I let you get away with that once. You won't get away with it again. So you just watch it! Porky-pudge!

LOTTIE *gives a bellow of fury and jams the salsa bowl down on* PENNY's *head.*

PENNY *rises and grabs* LOTTIE *and the two women grapple each other to the ground,* PENNY *lands on top of* LOTTIE. TEDDY, *after initial hesitation, weighs in to separate them.* REGGIE *stands back amazed.*

(during this, screaming) Porky-pudge! Porky-pudge! Porky-pudge! *(Etc.)*

LOTTIE *(during this, screaming)* Harlot! Whore! Hussy! *(Etc.)*

TEDDY *(during this, yelling)* Now, come on girls, break it up. Lottie! Penny! Break it up now! *(Etc.)*

TEDDY *manages to pull* PENNY *off* LOTTIE *and lifts her clear.* LOTTIE *takes the opportunity, whilst his back is to her, to pour a bowl of barbecue sauce over his head.* TEDDY *turns and tries to grab the bowl.* PENNY *grabs up a tray and hits him over the head with it.*

TEDDY's *knees buckle and he sits on the ground, dazed.* LOTTIE *tips a bowl of salad over his head.* PENNY *does likewise.* TEDDY *continues to sit there, covered in food. Both women step back to survey their handiwork.*

PENNY Ho-ho-ho-ho-ho...!

LOTTIE Ha-ha-ha-ha-ha...!

PENNY Another drink?

LOTTIE Why not?

They both go off towards the house. REGGIE, *who has remained well clear of things, watches them go.*

REGGIE Good grief!

He moves to TEDDY *who continues to sit there.*

You alright, old boy?

TEDDY *nods and grunts.*

You know it has to be said when it comes down to it, women are an extremely odd lot. Take a lot of understanding, don't you think? How does it go now? Men are from – somewhere or other and women are from somewhere completely different. Never a truer word.

TEDDY *continues to stare despairingly into space.*

You sure you're OK? You look a bit of a mess. Wrecked your shirt, I'm afraid. Lucky you had your apron on, eh?

TEDDY *(sudden realisation)* Oh, my god!

REGGIE What?

TEDDY The steaks! They'll be charred to a cinder! *(He half rises)*

REGGIE OK. OK. Stay there. I'll rescue them.

REGGIE *hurries round to open the barbecue.*

(surveying the interior) Ah! Hang on. Might be salvageable. Wait there.

He takes a couple of skewers and, after fiddling about inside emerges with a blackened object on the end of each skewer.

I think you might term these as being on the well done side.

He returns and sits on the ground by **TEDDY**, *handing him a skewer.*

There you go.

Both men sit and nibble the burnt offering.

Hmmm. Not bad. Not bad at all. Considering.

They eat a little more.

TEDDY It all depends on the quality of the meat.

REGGIE Oh, yes.

TEDDY You have to start with the right grade.

REGGIE Oh, rather...

TEDDY You need to have meat with good marbling.

REGGIE Oh, indeed.

TEDDY You also need to find a damn good butcher.

REGGIE Oh, yes. That's a must.

They eat a little more.

TEDDY I think this is completely inedible you know. *(He throws his skewer aside)*

REGGIE *(doing likewise)* Absolutely.

They sit. Slight pause.

Well, you know, I still haven't a clue what set those two off. Have you?

TEDDY *(getting up)* No idea, at all...

REGGIE *(getting up)* Closed book, old boy, women. Closed book.

They start to move off.

Tell you something though. Just to be on the safe side, in future, I'm going to give Uh-huh-huh-huh a bit of a wide berth.

TEDDY Same here, old boy, same here...

As they both go off the lights fade to a blackout.

End of Play

CHLOË WITH LOVE

The **BOTTLECAMP***'s garden in summer on a warm evening.*

Garden seating and a table or two.

LOTTIE, *small and anxious, enters with* **PENNY,** *tall and assured.*

PENNY *(as they enter)* ...yes, well they do, they tend to do that, Lottie, after a while. I mean, most men barely have an attention span of more than twenty minutes. So how on earth can you possibly hope to keep their attention after years of marriage. They're small children, most of them, darling. You have to keep poking your head round the corner of their pram and shouting "Boo!" at them. No, it's a sad fact of life. They all wander off eventually but with any luck you'll find they'll wander back again, provided you make it worth their while.

LOTTIE Does Reggie tend to do that? Wander off?

PENNY No. But then I tend to make it worth his while <u>not</u> to wander off. I work on the marital, high-voltage electric fence principle. If he tries to make a break he knows he'll be fried. No, Reggie's properly house-trained. I'm afraid with Teddy you've married a wanderer, darling.

LOTTIE Yes, I'm afraid I may have done. When he married me and promised to love me for ever, I couldn't believe my luck. Everyone was after him, you know...all we girls at St Olaf's. Do you remember, Penny, when he came to give that careers talk to the sixth forms. So handsome in his pinstripe suit and his blue tie...and those blazing eyes, so full of passion...

PENNY Oh, yes, I remember. A short history of lawn mowers, wasn't it? I'm afraid I gave that one a miss.

LOTTIE Oh, that was just the title. But there was so much
more than lawn mowers to his talk, Penny. The mowers
were just a metaphor.

PENNY A metaphor for what?

LOTTIE For everything. A metaphor for life. You see, we're all
of us just so many blades of grass, Penny, on Life's Lawn,
you see. We all have our brief moment of growth and then
finally we're all of us, the greatest down to the smallest,
we're all mown down and swept away into bins…

PENNY And turned into compost?

LOTTIE Even the greatest of us. No blade of grass, however
tall, is spared the mower. We all eventually turn brown,
shrivel and die.

PENNY Finally ending pushing up the daises? Completely
buggering up the lawn for next year, quite.

LOTTIE Oh, no, no. I know you're laughing at me, Penny. You are
so naughty! But if only you'd been there when Teddy talked.
All of us, hanging on his every word…he was completely
riveting. And he chose me. Of all the blades of grass on that
spring afternoon in that stuffy school hall…

PENNY It was you he plucked.

LOTTIE At the end, he called for questions. And no one was
putting their hand up, you see. I don't think anyone else
had the faintest clue what he was talking about, so in the
end I very timidly stuck my own hand up. It was so unlike
me to do that, it took tremendous courage, I can tell you.
And immediately he pointed straight at me and he said,
"Yes? That very attractive young lady, the one with the rosy
cheeks, right at the back there –" I was blushing like mad
you see, I always used to…

PENNY Yes, I remember.

LOTTIE …And I stumbled and stammered out something, asking
him what he considered was the optimum height for rotary

cutters for a first spring trimming – I made most of it up...
And then a few weeks later, in the holidays, he invited me
to lunch in his factory canteen. Gave me a guided tour
afterwards. He absolutely swept me off my feet. Until that
moment I never realised there were quite so many different
types of mower.

PENNY *(gently)* Yes it's a very romantic and touching story,
Lottie. And I love it more each time you tell it, darling. But
now it's all gone a teeny bit off course, hasn't it? And yes,
you've drifted a degree or two but I'm sure it's nothing too
serious, at present. But in my view, it's time you made a
few corrections to your navigation. Adjusted your marital
tiller. Because otherwise, believe me, given time you'll find
yourselves way off course. Leading eventually to one of you
abandoning ship. And I'm sure you don't want that.

LOTTIE *(distraught)* Oh, no, no. That would be my worst
nightmare, Penny. If Teddy left me, I don't know what I'd
do – I think I'd – just simply – I don't know what I'd – I
don't know!

PENNY Lottie! Lottie! Simmer down. Gently now. You mustn't
get yourself in a state, dear. Teddy's not going to leave you.

LOTTIE You're sure?

PENNY I promise. Teddy knows which – Teddy knows when
he's well off. He knows that, in you, he's found a treasure.
But if you want my advice, darling –

LOTTIE Oh, yes. I do, I really do need your advice, Penny, more
than anything! That's why I came to you. I always turn to
you. You know I do. You're my one and only best friend in
the world, aren't you? You know that.

PENNY I'm very fond of you too, Lottie.

LOTTIE Ever since you stood up for me at school with all those
awful bullies – the way they used to tease me with – with...

PENNY Porky-pudge!

LOTTIE Oh, God! Please don't even say it!

PENNY Sorry. That's all in the past. I mean look at you now. You're practically lissom. Practically.

LOTTIE You think so? I don't think I'd ever describe myself as lissom. Look, you see, I'm beginning to go, Penny, just round here, you see. But what can you do to stop it. The doctor said to me you can't fight gravity, Mrs Bulbin, it pulls us all down in the end –

PENNY Now Lottie! Now listen to me, Lottie! You need to buck your ideas up darling, you have developed a very negative self image and it is not helping you one tiny jot. You have to start saying to yourself over and over again, "I am attractive! I am a beautiful woman!" Over and over to yourself. Go on, Lottie! Say it! I am attractive... Come on, now!

LOTTIE *(tentatively)* I am attract – do you think I'm a beautiful woman, Penny?

PENNY Yes I do, Lottie. I most certainly do.

LOTTIE Thank you.

PENNY You may not be everyone's cup of tea but nonetheless. To a lot of people, you are drop dead gorgeous. As I'm sure you are to Teddy.

LOTTIE I was to Teddy. I was.

PENNY And will be again. Trust me. Listen, they'll be here soon. We're going upstairs to my bedroom. And I'm going to sit you down and give you a complete makeover –

LOTTIE *(alarmed)* Oh, God. I don't think I could face that –

PENNY Come on! Quick! Quick! Before they both come back!

LOTTIE Really, Penny – I never look good in too much make up...

PENNY That's because, darling, if you don't mind my saying so, on the rare occasions you do wear it, you layer it on with a trowel. Subtlety. Light brush strokes. Accentuate. Gentle shading here. Highlight here. I promise you a transformation.

LOTTIE *(breathlessly)* You think so?

PENNY I am a beautiful woman.

LOTTIE Yes you are, Penny.

PENNY No, darling, <u>you</u> are a beautiful woman. <u>You</u>! Now say it.

LOTTIE <u>I</u> am a beautiful woman.

PENNY Once more.

LOTTIE I am a beautiful –

A car horn sounds.

PENNY Listen, they've arrived. Quickly! Through the back way!

LOTTIE *(as they go)* I am a beautiful woman...

> **PENNY** *bundles* **LOTTIE** *off.*

> *A moment.*

> **TEDDY** *and* **REGGIE** *enter.*

> **TEDDY**, *assured and confident.*

> **REGGIE**, *his friend, slightly less so.*

> **REGGIE**, *the host, carries a bottle of wine on a tray with two glasses.*

REGGIE ...no they're not here. Must be in the house. Penny left these out ready. I presume they're to come down. We thought we'd have the pre-drinks out here. Penny decided we would, anyway.

TEDDY Lottie should have been here by now...

REGGIE Maybe they're up in the bedroom.

TEDDY Discussing shoes.

REGGIE Very probably.

TEDDY Or handbags. That's another favourite topic.

REGGIE Oh, my God. Handbags? Handbag chat? Can't tell you the number of handbag hours I've sat through with Penny. I don't know what you can possibly find to say about a handbag that can't be said in three sentences.

TEDDY One sentence is sufficient. Two word sentence. How much? Want me to go ahead and open this?

REGGIE Oh, please. If you'd be so kind.

TEDDY Better make a start on it, I suppose. *(Looking at the label)* Oh, this is good. This is good stuff. Very good.

REGGIE Oh, good.

TEDDY Yes! Very good indeed, this is.

REGGIE Good, good.

TEDDY Had a good few bottles of this in my time. All very good indeed.

REGGIE Well, the chap in the off license said it was good. Got it at a good price, too.

TEDDY Good man. Which off license you go to?

REGGIE Goodhews.

TEDDY Oh, yes they're pretty good news, Goodhews.

REGGIE I think they're pretty good, yes.

TEDDY Though probably not a patch on Goody's. Though they're a good distance away are Goody's. A good five miles away.

REGGIE Good heavens. That's a good distance.

TEDDY Worth it for a good bargain, though. They have a very good selection. *(Sniffing the glass)* Ah, yes! Good nose! Very good nose.

REGGIE Yes. Good.

TEDDY There you go!

He hands **REGGIE** *a glass.*

REGGIE Thanks.

TEDDY Good health!

REGGIE Good health!

They drink. **TEDDY** *sucks his wine noisily through his teeth, savouring it.*

TEDDY Oh, that is good.

REGGIE Good grief! Very good. Good bouquet, isn't it?

TEDDY *sucks noisily again.*

TEDDY Let the oxygen get to it. Just been opened, you see. Allow it to breathe.

REGGIE Yes, give it air, poor thing.

They both suck noisily.

TEDDY Good full body, hasn't it? Almonds...with just that hint of apricot. Can you taste it?

REGGIE Mmmm. Yes, I think I can taste pistachios. With overtones of prune.

TEDDY Yes, that as well. That as well. Plenty of prune in there. Gives it that full body.

REGGIE There's also some faint walnut somewhere.

TEDDY Probably. Keeps the peppermint company.

They savour their drinks. A silence.

No, it totally mystifies me how on earth women can chatter on together for hours on end about handbags.

REGGIE Goodness knows.

TEDDY Good health, old boy.

REGGIE Good health.

They sip and savour some more.

TEDDY So how's the motor industry? You still flogging those expensive cars of yours?

REGGIE Oh, not so bad. Can't complain.

TEDDY Amazed anybody's got any money left. These days.

REGGIE Oh, well, they're mostly foreigners buying them. These days.

TEDDY Ah, yes.

REGGIE But then they're mostly foreign cars, these days. Imported. So one shouldn't complain, I suppose.

TEDDY Fair enough.

REGGIE I mean, I'm just grateful they come here to buy them at all. Be far cheaper for most of them to stay at home and buy the bloody things there. Save them a load of money.

TEDDY They'll probably work that out eventually for themselves.

REGGIE Probably. Then no one will come here at all, will they? Have the place to ourselves, then.

TEDDY Damn sight quieter, I can tell you. Saturday night in Kidderminster. Mayhem, old boy. Of Babylonian proportions.

REGGIE Absolutely.

TEDDY *finishes his drink.*

TEDDY Can I help you to some more?

REGGIE Yes, I don't mind if I do, thank you. It's a bit more-ish this, isn't it?

TEDDY Very more-ish. Going to need a few bottles of this before the evening's out.

REGGIE Oh, yes, once Penny gets launched in...

TEDDY God, once she gets going, there'll be none left for us, will there? Never seen a woman put it away like Penny does.

REGGIE No, she keeps me busy, trotting up and down the cellar steps. It's OK, I bought a couple of cases.

TEDDY Good man. Fortunately Lottie doesn't drink very much. Not a big drinker. Can't hold it. She tends to fall over if she does. Where are they, for heaven's sake? Where've they both got to?

REGGIE No idea. Penny's probably pottering about somewhere. I presume Lottie's arrived by now. She was making her own way here, was she?

TEDDY She can hardly have got lost on the way, considering we live practically next door.

REGGIE Oh, don't worry, they'll be here. Penny's preparing something very light for supper. So it's not going to spoil if we're a bit late. We were going to eat out here but then these wretched midges... So we've compromised. We're going to have a cold collation in the dining room with both doors wide open. Then all we need to worry about are flies and the occasional wasp.

TEDDY Oh, you can always deal with those. Sitting targets compared to midges. Midges are like phantom jets.

REGGIE Fly under the radar?

TEDDY Or straight through the radar, quite often. Cheers. *(He takes another mouthful of wine)*

REGGIE *(doing likewise)* Cheers, old boy.

They sit contentedly, happy to enjoy each other's company for a moment.

You know, there's nothing nicer in this world, is there? Than sitting with someone you really know and like and have a lot in common with. And talk about things that really matter in life.

TEDDY Very true. Very, very true. You're right. This wine is very, very more-ish. Mind if I help myself?

REGGIE Carry on, old friend.

TEDDY Thank you.

TEDDY *gets up and retrieves the bottle.*

Perhaps you could give me a hand in finishing off the bottle?

REGGIE My pleasure.

He drains his glass and passes it to **TEDDY** *who drains the rest of the bottle into it.*

Plenty more where that came from.

TEDDY Splendid. I usually find the first bottle is little more than what tennis players term a warm up – it's not till the second one, that you really get the measure of the –

His mobile phone pings.

Oh, hang about, hang on. *(Fumbling in his pocket)* What's this? Excuse me.

He retrieves his phone and studies the screen.

Who on earth can this be?

REGGIE Not bad news, I hope.

TEDDY Hope not. I trust they've got better taste than to text me bad news.

REGGIE I don't know. A girl I knew once did that. Texted me. It just said, "Go way". That's all it said. "Go way".

TEDDY That was insensitive of her.

REGGIE I thought so. Upset me for hours...

TEDDY No, it's from Lottie. *(Reading)* "Held up. Meeting longer than expected." Only she's put exp'cted. "See you later. Ap'l'gies to all. L." I do so loathe these things, you know. People simply use them as an excuse for killing off the English language. All for the sake of two O's and an E. Thank God Shakespeare never had the use of text messaging.

REGGIE Been a lot shorter, if he had. The qlty of mcy is nt strnd. *(He laughs)*

TEDDY Meeting? I don't recall she ever said she was going to a meeting.

REGGIE Perhaps it's a secret meeting. A secret lover, perhaps? *(He laughs)*

TEDDY Not very secret, in that case, is he? If she's texting it. These text messages go everywhere. Via the CIA, MI5. No, Lottie never goes to meetings. She's not the meeting type. Not <u>meeting</u> meetings, anyway. She meets up with people occasionally. Usually with Penny. But she's not a woman you see popping up at meetings. Save the by-pass, that sort of thing.

REGGIE Mystery, then.

TEDDY Very. *(Raising his glass)* Here's looking at you, smiler.

REGGIE *(doing likewise)* And you.

They drink.

How are you both then? I haven't asked.

TEDDY *(somewhat darkly)* Oh, we're – alright. You know.

REGGIE Alright?

TEDDY Yes.

REGGIE Just alright? Sounds a bit bleak.

TEDDY Yes. Listen, Reggie, I have a spot of bother with Lottie. Frankly.

REGGIE Oh, dear... Having another of her funny turns, is she?

TEDDY No, no. She's fine. Well, she's sort of fine. As fine as Lottie can ever be. No, it's me. I should say, a spot of bother with <u>me</u> and Lottie.

REGGIE You?

TEDDY Yes.

REGGIE You're having funny turns?

TEDDY You know me, Reggie, better than anyone. You know what I used to be like. Before I married Lottie. Anything in a skirt, I was on to it.

REGGIE Lord, yes. I do remember. There was a time when you had three of them on the go at once, didn't you? One of them was mine.

TEDDY Yes, yes, don't bring all that up again. The point is, Reggie, I don't mean to sound vain or boastful but I was nothing short of irresistible, old boy. The plain fact is that women were swarming around me like wasps round a jam jar. There was nothing I could do to stop them. Till I was forced to take refuge, seek safe haven and married Lottie. And I made a solemn vow the day I married her. She was going to be my last one. For the rest of my life, my very last.

REGGIE Yes, I was in the church at the time. Standing behind you. I heard you say those very words.

TEDDY Lottie was to be the very last woman in my life. I truly meant that. And like a condemned man faced with his last meal, I was going to eke her out. Savour every mouthful.

REGGIE Beautifully put.

TEDDY And don't get me wrong, I've had some particularly fine meals at that particular restaurant, old boy. At Maison Lottie. You get my drift?

REGGIE Oh, yes. Cordon bleu.

TEDDY She may not be the looker, have the looks, but in the sack believe me, she's Michelin Star.

REGGIE Yes, well, she's got a jolly nice face. Friendly, you know. I rather go for friendly women. Prefer them to the grumpy ones. The ones that snarl at you, you know.

TEDDY Yes, well the point is, it had all been going swimmingly to plan, until lately...

REGGIE And?

TEDDY Lately, I've been getting – the old hunger pangs again.

REGGIE Seeking alternative cuisine?

TEDDY More or less. I'm beginning to wander again. In search of fresh watering holes. And, the point is, I think Lottie's beginning to suspect. She's starting to give me fishy looks over breakfast.

REGGIE Oh, dear.

TEDDY The fact is, I'm frightfully fond of her, she's a wonderful woman in many respects –

REGGIE She is.

TEDDY And frankly I don't know what I'd do, what would become of me, if she ever gave me the elbow.

REGGIE Oh, that's unthinkable. You and Lottie, Lottie and you, you're – chalk and cheese – no – peas in a pod, rather...

TEDDY The fact is that I badly need to keep on the straight and narrow.

REGGIE ...bubble and squeak. Steak and kidney...

TEDDY And I'm going to need your help to do that.

REGGIE Sage and onion... Sorry? You're going to need my what?

TEDDY I'm going to need your help, Reggie. To keep me on the straight and narrow. If you see me starting to wander off into the rough, just be there to shoo me back on to the fairway.

REGGIE Shoo you back?

TEDDY Just say to me, "Teddy, remember Lottie! You belong together. You belong together like –"

REGGIE Cheese and biscuits?

TEDDY Exactly. In the final resort if it comes down to it, you're at liberty to use force if required. Force. If required. You hear?

REGGIE Force? On you?

TEDDY You have my full permission. Pull me away and hold me down.

REGGIE Screw the lid back on the jam jar?

TEDDY Exactly so.

REGGIE What about her? What about the wretched woman? What if she continues to swarm?

TEDDY Well, swat her away, Reggie, swat her away! God, if I lost Lottie, now, you know... *(Getting rather tearful)* ...I don't know what I'd do, old boy, I really don't... I don't know what on earth I'd do...

REGGIE *(rising)* Easy, easy Teddy. Easy old boy. You're not going to lose Lottie. Lottie? No way. Never! Not while I'm here. Not while you've got me, Teddy. Come on now, pull yourself together.

TEDDY *(regaining some composure)* Sorry... I'm so sorry... Suddenly saw my life stretching out in front of me like some endless – meaningless motorway...

REGGIE Possibly the M5. Listen, Teddy, I'm going to fetch us another bottle of this, cheer us up. See if I can rout out Penny. You sit there and take deep breaths, old boy...

TEDDY *(rising, alarmed)* No, don't leave me here alone! Please, don't leave me, Reggie!

REGGIE No, of course not. No. You can come along, too.

TEDDY Thank you so much. Anyway, I need the – I'm in need of the – of the –

REGGIE Yes, of course. You can use the downstairs one...come on old chap.

TEDDY *(as they go)* Thank you, old friend. I couldn't face sitting there, all on my own. Just me and the midges...

REGGIE Come on, then. This way.

They go off. A pause.

From the other direction, **PENNY** *and* **LOTTIE** *return.* **LOTTIE** *is completely transformed, almost unrecognisable.*

PENNY, *in the brief time at her disposal, has wrought miracles to her friend's appearance with clothes, makeup and even a rather exotic wig she had in her collection. Whether the end result is actually preferable to the original is debatable but nonetheless this new* LOTTIE *certainly presents a woman who, in vulgar parlance, is clearly up for it.*

LOTTIE I'm not happy with this at all, Penny, I'm really not...

PENNY Nonsense, Lottie, I keep telling you, you look fabulous.

LOTTIE All this just isn't me. It's simply not <u>me</u>, Penny.

PENNY Well, that's the whole point, isn't it? It's not you, is it? You're Chloë. You're my old school friend, Chloë, remember?

LOTTIE Chloë? I can't even recall a Chloë...

PENNY Because she never really existed. Till now. Now, this is Chloë. And she's a knockout.

LOTTIE Why Chloë, for goodness' sake? Do I have to be a Chloë? I don't feel a Chloë.

PENNY No, but you look a Chloë. Now you have to be a Chloë, darling.

LOTTIE It's all so deceitful. Sending him text messages. Deceiving him, like this. I've never deceived Teddy. I've never lied to him, never, during the whole of our marriage.

PENNY Well, it's about time you started, dear. He's been deceiving you, from all accounts, hasn't he? Be honest, now.

LOTTIE Possibly. Possibly he has. I don't know. Anyway, he'll recognise me, as soon as he looks at me. I know he will. I'm his wife, for heaven's sake!

PENNY Darling, be honest. How often has Teddy looked at you lately as his wife. Really looked at you? How often?

LOTTIE Well, he glances at me occasionally, now and then. Enough to remember what I look like. Though, come to think of it, I did have my hair recoloured and completely re-styled the other week and he didn't notice the difference for days and days. So...

PENNY My point, precisely.

LOTTIE But looking like this, he is going to look at me. He's certainly going to look at Chloë, isn't he?

PENNY I sincerely hope so. If he's male and at all red-blooded, he'll certainly give you a second glance. You're like catnip.

LOTTIE Then he'll see it's me. He'll see straight through me.

PENNY Well in that case, as soon as he suspects that under all that, it's you, his beloved Lottie, then you can expose yourself.

LOTTIE Oh, my God!

PENNY Behold, it is I, Teddy! Beneath this paint and powder, these superficial trimmings, it is I, your own true Lottie. And then you'll kiss him and hug him tightly – or whatever it is you normally do with Teddy...

LOTTIE *(shyly)* Well, we usually stroke each other's bottoms. He rather likes it when I do that...

PENNY Yes, spare me the details, darling. You can have all the fun in the world together the moment you both get home. The point is this whole exercise is designed to kick start your marriage... Which appears to have stalled. Like one of Reggie's wretched vehicles...

LOTTIE What about Reggie? What if Reggie recognises me?

PENNY Reggie barely recognises anybody. He stands in front of the mirror some mornings looking faintly puzzled.

LOTTIE Oh, but what if he fancies Chloë? Rather than Teddy? What happens then?

PENNY Trust me. If that happens, leave me to deal with Reggie. I can deal with that, don't worry. Where the hell are they, anyway?

LOTTIE I don't think I can go through with this Penny, I really don't.

PENNY Come along, Lottie, you can do it! Why I can remember you in the school play. You were brilliant! What was her name, now?

LOTTIE You mean Vanda the Vamp?

PENNY Vanda the Vamp! You were wonderful! Just imagine Chloë as Vanda.

LOTTIE But that was just a play and anyway –

Offstage chuntering.

PENNY Oh, look they're coming...they're coming... Be Chloë, remember! You're Chloë!

LOTTIE Chloë! Chloë!

REGGIE, *carrying a fresh bottle of wine, returns, followed by* TEDDY.

REGGIE *(as they enter)* Ah, you're here!

PENNY Where have you been, for heaven's sake?

REGGIE Sorry, we must have kept missing each other. We kept going in one door while you were coming out the – *(Catching his first glimpse of* LOTTIE *as Chloë)* Oh! Oh, I say!

PENNY We've been looking for you everywhere. I wanted you to meet an old school friend of mine. This is my friend, Chloë.

REGGIE Oh, hallo...

TEDDY *(sensing trouble ahead)* Oh, my God.

PENNY Chloë, this is my husband Reggie.

LOTTIE *(as Chloë)* Hello, Weggie!

PENNY And this is Reggie's very best friend, Teddy Bulbin.

LOTTIE *(as Chloë, employing a strange, untraceable accent)* Pleathed to meet you, Mithter Bulbin... *(She flashes him a dazzling smile)*

TEDDY *(already captivated)* Oh, please. Do call me Teddy.

LOTTIE *(as Chloë)* Teddy! I've been dying to meet you. Penny's told me tho much about you.

TEDDY *(laughing)* Has she really? What's she been saying about me?

LOTTIE *(as Chloë)* Only nice things, I pwomith.

REGGIE I bet she hasn't mentioned me.

PENNY No, Reggie, I haven't mentioned you and I don't intend to. Now then, what are we all having? Oh good, you've brought the wine. Splendid. Now all we need, we girls, is a glass to drink it from. Reggie, darling, be an angel and fetch us two more glasses.

REGGIE *(reluctant to leave)* – er...

PENNY Chloë's really desperate to meet Teddy. She has this passion for lawn mowers, you know. Practically an obsession. Now, I insist you two sit there together. And I'll pour us a glass – Reggie!

REGGIE What?

PENNY Run along! Fetch the glasses, darling!

REGGIE Glasses? Right. You'll be OK, Teddy, will you? I'm just fetching a couple of glasses.

TEDDY *(his full attention on* **LOTTIE***)* Yes, OK. Just as you like.

REGGIE *(pointedly)* I'm sure your wife, Lottie, will be here in a minute. Remember Lottie. Lottie.

PENNY Reggie. Go!

REGGIE *goes off rather reluctantly.*

Right. Don't mind me, you two. You carry on. I'll just sit and look at the view. I haven't seen it for a while.

TEDDY I hear you're interested in mowers, Chloë? That's unusual.

LOTTIE *(as Chloë)* I find mowerth quite fathcinating. I know it's thilly but...

TEDDY No, no, no. Nothing silly about mowers. Serious business mowers, in my line anyway. No, it's just unusual to find a woman who's keen on them. Mowing, in my experience, is a particularly masculine pastime. Mowing and men, they seem to go together...

LOTTIE *(as Chloë)* One man went to mow... *(She laughs)*

TEDDY Yes, got it in one! Now, women, I tend to think more in terms of weeding. Women and weeding, rather than mowing. That seems a more natural combination.

LOTTIE *(as Chloë)* Oh, yes I weed masses. I'm forever weeding.

TEDDY Ah, there you go, you see.

LOTTIE *(as Chloë)* I weed mainly womantic novels but the occasional biogwaphies...

TEDDY *(laughing)* No, no, I think we may be at cross purposes here...

LOTTIE *(as Chloë)* Cwoss purposeth... Yeth. How thilly. *(She laughs)*

TEDDY *(laughing)* Very thilly!

PENNY Oh, dear God! Was this a good idea?

> **REGGIE** *rushes back in with two glasses.*

REGGIE *(slightly breathless)* Sorry to be so long, everyone!

LOTTIE *(as Chloë)* Oh, look here's Weggie!

PENNY You were quick.

REGGIE Yes, sorry to be so quick, everyone. How are you doing, Teddy?

TEDDY Wasps are beginning to swarm, old boy.

REGGIE Oh, lord.

TEDDY Better start screwing the old lid back on the jam jar, pretty quickly.

REGGIE OK, help is at hand, old boy.

PENNY What are you both talking about? Wasps?

LOTTIE *(as Chloë)* I don't like wathps. They thting you.

REGGIE Right-ho! Here we go! What are we all having? Penny, darling, wine for you?

PENNY Thank you.

TEDDY You know, I'm intrigued, Chloë, by your accent. Where do you come from originally?

LOTTIE *(as Chloë)* Well, I'm owiginally from Waleth.

TEDDY Wales! I'd never have guessed that.

PENNY I don't think anybody would have done.

LOTTIE *(as Chloë)* But I'm just a teenist bit Thcottish on my thister'th thide.

REGGIE *(inveigling himself between them)* Here you are, Chloë. Get that down you.

LOTTIE *(as Chloë)* Thank you, Weggie.

REGGIE Cheers! You don't mind if I sit between you, do you? *(Sitting between them)* Thank you.

LOTTIE *(as Chloë)* We thertainly do. We're buthy discussing mowerth.

REGGIE Really? Mowerth? Well, it's a good night to see them. Soon as it's dark enough, they'll be attracted to the garden lights, swarms of them...

LOTTIE *(as Chloë)* No, not moths. I mean mowerth. Lawn mowerth.

PENNY Reggie! Come away from there!

REGGIE Sorry, darling, just a second. We're having this very interesting conversation...

LOTTIE *(as Chloë)* Yes, Weggie, do go way, I want to talk to Teddy. You thee, Teddy, I believe our whole life is like a lawn, don't you? We're all of us little bladth of gwath waiting for the final mower. Waiting to cut uth down into the gweat gwath bin in the thky...

TEDDY Chloë, we are twin souls. I share your feelings, my dear...

REGGIE Talking of mowers, I don't know if Penny told you, Chloë. But I'm in cars myself. Top of the range, largely imported. Does that interest you at all?

LOTTIE *(as Chloë)* No. I hate carth. Nathty smelly thingth. Do go away!

PENNY Reggie, come over here. Leave them to talk.

LOTTIE *(as Chloë)* Yeth. Weggie. Do pleathe pith off.

> **REGGIE** *returns reluctantly to* **PENNY**.

> *Chloë draws closer to* **TEDDY**.

REGGIE *(to* **PENNY**, *confidentially)* Darling, I can't possibly leave them.

PENNY *(quietly)* Why on earth not?

REGGIE *(quietly)* Because, for one thing, the jam jar's still wide open. That woman's about to eat Teddy alive.

PENNY *(quietly)* Alright, then, let her. Just keep out of it!

> **TEDDY** *and* **LOTTIE** *have drawn closer and closer. They are on the brink of kissing.*

REGGIE Oh, God. No, I'm sorry, I can't stand by and watch this happen. I'm sorry. *(With a yell)* Teddy!

TEDDY *(startled)* What?

REGGIE Don't do it, old boy! Remember your vow. Think of Lottie! *(Loudly)* Lottie! Lottie! Lottie!

LOTTIE *(irritably)* Yes? Yes? What? *(As Chloë)* I mean yeth?

TEDDY Yes. Think of Lottie. *(He pulls away)* Lottie, Lottie. Excuse me, Chloë, I need to get a refill.

TEDDY *moves to the table, his back momentarily to* LOTTIE. *He pours himself another glass.* LOTTIE *rises and moves beside him.*

LOTTIE *(as Chloë)* Yeth, I think I could jutht manage a thmall one, too.

REGGIE *(brightly, watching them anxiously)* Talking of Wales, Chloë, my grandmother on my mother's side was slightly Irish you know –

PENNY Oh, Reggie, do shut up.

LOTTIE *(as Chloë) (leaning in close to* TEDDY*)* Yes, shut up Weggie! *(To* TEDDY*)* You've got vewwy stwong handth, I must thay... That mutht be all the mowing...

REGGIE Old gran used to sing us traditional lullabies, you know...

TEDDY Well, I don't personally do much mowing myself, these days. Leave that to the sales team. I'm mainly desk work...

LOTTIE *(as Chloë, pressing close to* TEDDY*)* Weally? I love dethkth, too.

PENNY She's gone completely batty.

REGGIE You're telling me, where the hell did you find her? More important, where the hell is Lottie?

PENNY Heaven knows, she's in there, somewhere.

REGGIE *(mystified)* What?

At this point, LOTTIE *starts running her hand over* TEDDY*'s bottom. He reacts, violently.*

TEDDY Oh, my God! For God's sake don't do that, woman!

LOTTIE *(as Chloë)* Don't you find it thensual? I do. You can wub mine, too, if you like.

TEDDY Oh my God, Reggie, somebody help me! She's discovered my Achilles' heel!

REGGIE It doesn't look like that from here, old boy. You stop doing that at once! That type of thing's way below the belt, you loose, sinful – thing!

PENNY Reggie!

LOTTIE *(as Chloë, angrily)* Don't you call me thinful!

REGGIE *(angrily)* You are, you're thinful! You're little thort of thinful!

PENNY Reggie!

LOTTIE *(as Chloë, angrily)* I'm not thinful, I'm thexy!

REGGIE Oh, you think so do you? Well let me tell you, young woman, there's a very fine line between thinful and thexy and you've just – thtepped over it!

PENNY Reggie! Leave them alone, at once!

REGGIE I can't leave them alone, can I?

TEDDY *has started responding and begun stroking* LOTTIE*'s bottom.*

I mean, look at them. It's like Sodom and Gomorrah over there!

PENNY Reggie, go and fetch the nibbles! They're on the kitchen table!

REGGIE Nibbles? How can you think of nibbles, woman, at a time like this?

PENNY *(loudly and fiercely)* Reggie! Go and fetch them, at once!

REGGIE Alright! Alright! But I'll be back, I promise! Teddy, old chum, try and hold out a minute or two longer. I'm going to fetch the nibbles.

TEDDY *(in a frenzy)* Nipples? My God! Did you say nipples?

He starts mauling LOTTIE *with renewed fervour.*

REGGIE Oh, no! The chap's hovering on a knife edge.

PENNY *(fiercely)* Reggie!

REGGIE Alright! I'm going! I'm going! Wait there!

> **REGGIE** *goes off at a canter.*

> **TEDDY** *and* **LOTTIE** *are now entwined and kissing passionately.*

LOTTIE *(as Chloë, coming up for air)* Oh, you're thexy! You're tho, tho thexy...

TEDDY Tho are you.

LOTTIE *(as Chloë, drawing him away)* Letth have thex on the gwath, thall we? ...thex on the gwath...?

TEDDY ...yeth...thex on the gwath...

PENNY Chloë! Chloë, dear!

LOTTIE *(as Chloë)* We'll be like little bladeth of gwass...

PENNY Chloë! Chloë!

LOTTIE *(as Chloë)* Yeth?

PENNY I think it's time to reveal yourself, don't you?

LOTTIE *(as Chloë)* Thowwy? *(Sorry?)*

PENNY I think it's time to expose yourself...

TEDDY Yes, I think it's probably about that time, isn't it?

PENNY Chloë! Tell him!

LOTTIE Oh, right. Hallo, Teddy. It's me, Teddy.

TEDDY Yes, I know who you are, you're... Chloë... *(Slightly bemused)* Aren't you?

LOTTIE No, It's me. Lottie. It's Lottie, Teddy.

TEDDY Lottie? *(Peering closely at her)* Oh, good grief. So it is. Lottie. What are you –? Why are you –? Oh my, God. I'm terribly sorry. I do apologise. I thought you were somebody else.

LOTTIE Are you disappointed?

TEDDY What?

LOTTIE That it's me?

TEDDY Oh, no, no...

LOTTIE Would you have preferred someone else, Teddy? If I'd been someone else?

TEDDY No, no, Lottie. It's always been you, old girl. You're number one, you know that.

PENNY moves towards the house.

PENNY *(making a discreet exit)* I'll just go and see if Reggie needs a hand.

PENNY *exits.*

The others barely notice her departure, their attention still on each other.

TEDDY But, Lottie, why on earth are you dressed up like this – what's with all the disguise, old girl?

LOTTIE I was just trying to re-awaken your interest. In me. Stir your passion.

TEDDY Oh, come on. I've never lost interest. Not in you.

LOTTIE I think you have, you know, Teddy. Just a tiny bit. I mean, just now we were kissing passionately and you didn't even know it was me, did you?

TEDDY I had an innate instinct...that it could have been. Possibly, someone like you...but... No, I didn't, Lottie. But fair do's, it's been some time since we've done that, you and I, isn't it?

LOTTIE My point exactly.

TEDDY I mean, you didn't have to go to these lengths, surely? You could just have changed your hair style or something, if you wanted to attract my attention, surely?

LOTTIE Teddy, I've changed my hair style so many times over the past months. I've had it coloured, re-coloured, permed, straightened so often, Maurice says it's practically falling out.

TEDDY Well, don't go bald on my account, will you? No, you were very good, Lottie. As Chloë.

LOTTIE Did you like her?

TEDDY Yes, I did rather. Rather attractive.

LOTTIE And now you know she's me?

TEDDY Even more attractive now.

LOTTIE Maybe I could even be her again? From time to time?

TEDDY That'd be fun?

LOTTIE *(as Chloë)* Would you find that thexy, Teddy bear?

TEDDY Oh, yes, you bet. Very thexy.

They kiss deeply.

LOTTIE *(as Chloë)* Thex on the gwass, then?

TEDDY Thertainly. Thex on the gwass it is.

They start to undress each other. TEDDY *removes* LOTTIE*'s dress. He tosses it aside.* LOTTIE *unfastens* TEDDY*'s trousers. She tosses them aside. They stand together in their underwear.*

LOTTIE This is fun.

TEDDY Yes. Great fun. *(Taking both her hands)* Come on then. Nice patch of lawn over here...

As they start to move off, REGGIE *enters with two bowls of nibbles. He sees them and reacts.*

REGGIE Oh, dear God! In the nick of time.

REGGIE *strides forward and pulls* LOTTIE *away from* TEDDY.

Unhand that man, at once, woman!

LOTTIE Don't do that! How dare you!

TEDDY Steady on, old boy!

LOTTIE *and* **REGGIE** *wrestle together.*

REGGIE *(struggling with her)* You keep your hands off my friend, you loose harpy – you Jezebel, you strumpet of Babylon...

LOTTIE *(struggling with him)* Don't you call me a strumpet, you common little car salesman!

REGGIE How dare you call me a car salesman! I'm an executive sales director...

They both crash to the ground.

TEDDY *(standing back, ineffectually)* Hey! Hey! Hey! Steady now, you two!

LOTTIE *(furiously, as they fight)* Salesman!

REGGIE		*(furiously)* Strumpet!
LOTTIE	*(speaking together)*	*(furiously)* Salesman!
REGGIE		*(furiously)* Strumpet!

TEDDY *(without lifting a finger)* Come on now, chaps! Break it up!

REGGIE *has* **LOTTIE** *pinned to the ground. He manages to hold her. They are both breathless.*

REGGIE Now you just simmer down, you hear? You slithering serpent!

LOTTIE *(struggling to free herself)* You let go of me you – *(Yelling)* Help! Somebody! Help! I'm being molested by a common car salesman! Help! Teddy! Do something! Help me! Teddy, please!

TEDDY Easy on, old boy. Don't squash her.

REGGIE No use calling for him, you snake in the grass! You've got to deal with me, first!

LOTTIE Teddy! Somebody! Help! He's mad!

They continue struggling on the ground, REGGIE *still on top.* TEDDY, *rather conscious of his semi-naked state, steps forward and half-heartedly tries to separate the two of them.*

TEDDY *(as he does so)* Now, you two, come along...

PENNY *re-enters. She takes in the situation.*

PENNY What on earth's going on?

TEDDY Oh, God!

TEDDY *takes refuge behind the nearest chair, holding it up as a shield to preserve his modesty.*

PENNY Reggie! Stop that! Reggie! Teddy, what's happening? Stop them! For God's sake stop them! Teddy, do something!

TEDDY Sorry, Penny, I seem to have mislaid my kit.

REGGIE It's alright, darling, leave this to me. Everything's under control!

PENNY *(in her best dog handler's tone)* Reggie! Off! Off! Off her, Reggie. Down, Reggie! Get down, at once! Bad, Reggie! *(Finally giving up)* Oh, for God's sake!

She snatches up a tray and clouts REGGIE *on the head with it, knocking him cold. He goes limp and* LOTTIE *manages to wriggle free of him and retrieves her dress which she clasps to her.*

There! Supper's on the table, everyone!

LOTTIE *(reproachfully)* Teddy. You just stood there. You did nothing. You did nothing to save me.

TEDDY Yes, I'm sorry, old love. I was just a bit – incommoded...

LOTTIE So was I. He was – he was going to – he was just about to –

PENNY No, Lottie. I don't think he was you know. Not Reggie. Not at all.

LOTTIE No?

PENNY Trust me, that's not in Reggie's nature. Believe me, he's someone who needs an awful lot of coaxing first... Gentle encouragement. You need to wait ages and ages before he even...

REGGIE gives a groan.

Oh, good. He's back with us again. Now, do come along, everyone, before the baked potatoes get cold. *(Extending a hand)* Lottie? Come on, darling, you can get dressed indoors. You coming, Teddy? Tell Reggie we're in the dining room, will you?

TEDDY Yes, of course. I just need to get my trousers on again, if you don't mind. If I can find them. Make an effort to dress for dinner, anyway. *(He laughs rather feebly)*

The women both smile back at him frostily.

PENNY *(coolly)* Yes, trousers would be greatly appreciated...

LOTTIE *(coolly)* Makes no difference to me frankly, Teddy, whether they're on or off.

They leave.

TEDDY locates his trousers and starts putting them on again.

REGGIE sits up dizzily.

REGGIE *(shaking his head)* Lord!

TEDDY You alright, are you?

REGGIE What happened there? The sky fell in.

TEDDY No, it was Penny.

REGGIE Penny?

TEDDY She hit you on the head with the tray.

REGGIE Oh, did she? She's always doing that.

TEDDY She is?

REGGIE Whenever we have a disagreement, it usually ends up with her hitting me on the head with something or other. Still that's marriage for you, isn't it? The problem is, as is frequently the case on such occasions, I haven't the faintest idea what we were disagreeing about. Still, no doubt she will tell me in the course of time.

TEDDY Probably.

REGGIE Has Lottie arrived, yet?

TEDDY Yes, she's – just put in an appearance.

REGGIE Oh, my God! *(Getting up)* Then, where's that terrible woman – Zoe – Chloë – I hope she's gone?

TEDDY Oh, yes. There's just Lottie here now.

REGGIE Oh, thank God. The other one's gone for good, I trust?

TEDDY Chloë? Probably. *(Rather sadly)* No, I don't think we'll be seeing her again, somehow.

REGGIE Well, there's no need to look so sad about it, old boy. Cheer up! Got your twowthers on, have you?

TEDDY *(smiling)* Yes, I've got my twowthers on.

> **REGGIE** *puts an arm round* **TEDDY**'s *shoulders.*

REGGIE *(as they start to leave)* Then let's go and have a thpot of thupper, shall we?

TEDDY *(going off)* Thplendid, old boy, thplendid!

> *As they leave, the lights fade. Blackout.*

End of Play

PROPS

Drinks (p9)
Half-full red wine bottle (p9)
Barbecue (p10)
Barbecue briquettes (p11)
Firelighters (p13)
Glasses (p17)
Tray laden with uncooked food including marinated steaks (p19)
Second tray (p20)
Oiling the grill from a small bowl of vegetable oil with a brush (p22)
Lettuce (p23)
Chair (p25)
Bowl of mayonnaise (p30)
Bowl of salsa (p30)
Bowl of barbecue sauce (p31)
Bottle of wine on tray with two glasses (p41)
Mobile phone (p46)
Fresh bottle of wine (p53)
Two glasses (p55)
Two bowls of nibbles (p62)

LIGHTING

Lights fade to a blackout (p33)
Lights fade to a blackout (p66)

SOUND EFFECTS

Mobile phone 'ping' (p46)

VISIT THE SAMUEL FRENCH BOOKSHOP AT THE ROYAL COURT THEATRE

Browse plays and theatre books, get expert advice and enjoy a coffee

Samuel French Bookshop
Royal Court Theatre
Sloane Square
London
SW1W 8AS
020 7565 5024

Shop from thousands of titles on our website

 samuelfrench.co.uk

 samuelfrenchltd

 samuel french uk